On the
The Sinking of the 'Belgrano'

On the Spot

The Sinking of the 'Belgrano'

by Diana Gould

Introduction by Tam Dalyell MP

CECIL WOOLF · LONDON

First published 1984
©1984 Diana S. Gould; Introduction © 1984 Tam Dalyell

Cecil Woolf Publishers, 1 Mornington Place, London NW1 7RP
Tel: 01-387 2394

ISBN 0-900821-71-X paperback edition
ISBN 0-900821-72-8 hardback edition

Contents

Introduction by Tam Dalyell	page 7
On the Spot	11
Part I: Background	
Cambridge and After	14
Cirencester and Tewkesbury Constituency	19
1982	22
The Task Force	24
War	27
The Aftermath	30
Part II: The Franks Report	
1965-1979	32
1979-1982	35
Part III: 1983 Election Year	
Cotswold Town and Country	44
'Hansard'	46
An Election is Called	49
The Letter	51
May 24th 1983	55
Not an Election Issue?	61
Correspondence	64
'Six Hours Away with Exocets'	68
A Young Man's Death	71
The Sunday Papers	73
Post-Election	77

Introduction

To coincide with the Edinburgh International Music and Drama Festival, it has now become a tradition to stage a 'TV Festival'. Broadcasters and critics flock to BBC Scotland's studios to contemplate and scrutinise their own performance. Many of the heavyweights of British broadcasting and journalism participate. In August and September 1983, it was natural that one of the sessions should be devoted to an assessment of television coverage of the General Election, some eleven weeks earlier. Paul Fox, the Chairman of Yorkshire Television invited my wife and me to be guests at this particular session. If I mention that we sat up in the balcony, from which no one normally participates in the conference discussion, it is because this trivial fact had piquant relevance to what occurred later.

In the Festival Brochure, the introduction to the session on the General Election had been written by Peter Kellner, Political Editor of the *New Statesman*. He opened his piece by stating that the highlight to the General Election for him came at 6.40 one summer's evening during the campaign when Mrs Diana Gould, a housewife in Cirencester, cross-questioned Mrs Thatcher on the sinking of the *General Belgrano*. Kellner went on to assert that on no other occasion during the campaign was Mrs Thatcher rattled.

Three politicians made introductory speeches: Roy Hattersley spoke for Labour, David Steel for the Alliance and Tom King for the Conservatives. King made the observation in his opening remarks that the Mrs Gould, referred to in his programme, was a 'stooge'—'Tam Dalyell in drag,' said he. Being a guest, I said nothing, though I thought it highly offensive. Then, on a giant-sized screen, they showed the remarkable confrontation which was to become the genesis of this book. I had not seen it before, though it had generated a powerful leading article in *The Guardian*. But I vividly remembered canvassing that May evening in the Linlithgow Constituency, to be told at door after door, 'Did you see yon woman about yon ship with Thatcher on the telly just now? You should ha' seen her. She was great. Had Thatcher in some tizzy.' 'Yon woman,' who had made such an electric impression on my constituents was Mrs Diana Gould.

But back to the BBC studios in Edinburgh in the early autumn of 1983. A high proportion of the mandarins of journalism duly assembled had been busy during the election and had not seen that astonishing Nationwide either. Seeing the replay, they gasped. They hooted at the Prime Minister's answers. They giggled at her patent discomforture. They jeered at her diaphanous answers. Then the lights went up and there was further acid comment on the wholly unconvincing nature of the Prime Minister's response, with some references to the fact that Mrs Gould was obviously a stooge set up by Mrs Thatcher's opponents.

This was more than I could take. Provoked by the disparaging references to Mrs Gould, I could contain myself no longer. So, as one newspaper put it, 'Mr Dalyell leaned over the balcony and, *deus ex machina*, announced himself.' The result was a startled hush and a captive audience, craning their necks to see what occurred, twisting themselves round in astonished silence.

'I'm Tam Dalyell and I just want to make two points. First of all, Mrs Diana Gould was *not* my stooge. I have no notion of her political affiliation, if indeed she is a member of any political party. Like many others, Mrs Gould wrote to me, asking for information about the sinking of the

Belgrano, about which I had had masses to say publicly. As with everyone else who wrote, I sent her references to *Hansard*, where Ministers had responded to my many questions. I did not 'put Mrs Gould up to it,' though it may have given her confidence in tackling Mrs Thatcher on television to have had Parliamentary answers in front of her. Secondly, how come that you people in your own TV conference accord such importance to this incident that you highlight it in your programme and replay it here in Edinburgh, and yet you did not see fit to follow it up at the time? Not necessarily to get the answers that Tam Dalyell wanted, but to establish the truth? Was it not your professional duty to do so? And you, Robin, you know perfectly well that you have opportunities during a General Election to follow up a Prime Minister, once, twice, three times, four times, that *I* never have in the House of Commons!'

As *The Daily Mail* felicitously put it, Day rounded on Dalyell 'like a wounded ox'. He blurted out that Michael Foot had told him that he would have done the same thing and sunk the *Belgrano* and that it was not an election issue. (On what previous occasion, one might wonder, did Robin Day dutifully take the word of the Leader of the Opposition that a topic was not an election issue?) Mr Hattersley had the wit to ask *when* Michael Foot had made any such statement — adding that since Day had implied that he had been told 'in confidence' by Foot, he would never trust Day with any of his, Hattersley's, confidences.

The press concentrated the following day on Robin Day's gaffe in relation to the breach or alleged breach of confidence with Michael Foot. Much more important, however, is the question of why Mrs Gould's historic clash was not followed up. It amounts to a flagrant dereliction of duty on the part of the media.

I believe that there are two different explanations. The first is that Diana Gould did what no commentator or politician could have got away with, faced by a Prime Minister. She could not be bullied or dismissed. As one of my senior colleagues put it, 'Thatcher can bully Day, but she is not going to gain by being perceived to bully a West Country housewife.' In addition, the same Diana Gould, judging by her demeanour, is not going to be bullied by any soul, Prime Minister or not. By any standards, the sheer coolness of her performance was most unusual. Secondly, the British media and public cannot bring themselves to believe the sheer enormity of the charges against Mrs Margaret Hilda Thatcher: that she is guilty of gross deception, of lying to the House of Commons and, implicitly, of calculated murder for her own domestic political ends. British Prime Ministers simply don't behave like that, do they, old boy? It was Mrs Gould who established in the popular mind the impression that the sinking of the *Belgrano*, at best, was 'not cricket'. When a Public Enquiry under the 1921 Tribunal of Enquiry (Evidence) Act finally comes — as surely it must with the unfolding events — much of the credit will belong to this remarkable lady from Cirencester. She sowed the seed of doubt in the popular imagination, in a way that neither I nor any other politician could have done.

Tam Dalyell

On the Spot

The phone rang just as I was about to pour out the coffee; 'This is "Nationwide". Will you appear on our programme on Tuesday and put your question to Mrs Thatcher?'

I was literally struck dumb! After a silence my first words were: 'But you do not know anything about me!'

The caller, Julie Haden, then began again and verified that I had written a letter to 'Nationwide' with the heading 'The Lost Hours'. In the course of our conversation it became clear that when I wrote the letter I had no idea that they were about to produce a direct question-and-answer programme, and now indeed I was the one on the spot.

Julie told me that from my letter the programme producers felt I certainly knew my facts and had explained them very clearly. She said that it was by way of being a preliminary phone call and that she would ring again the following evening, Friday, 20 May 1983.

Still feeling dazed I took the coffee through to the living-room where my husband was relaxing after our evening meal and watching the television. My extraordinary news rather shattered the peace and we discussed what I should do.

'Have you the courage of your convictions?' was what he asked.

We examined the likely outcome of my appearing on

the programme, including the loss of privacy and the distinct possibility of being subjected to abuse. I decided to take my courage in both hands and go ahead and accept the invitation, if indeed it was still offered to me the following evening.

Since 24 May many people have contacted me, wanting me to form a pressure group to attempt to force the Government to order a full inquiry into the sinking of the *Belgrano* and its effect on the escalation of the Falklands war. I did not feel able to do this, but I have written my account in the hope that any publicity it gains will help those in Parliament who seek such an inquiry.

Part I
Background

Cambridge and After

My interest in the Falkland Islands went back a long way. As a student of Geography at Cambridge in the mid-1940s I had the privilege of learning from and getting to know Professor Frank Debenham. He was then nearing retirement as Professor of Geography. As is well known he went when a young man as geologist on Scott's last expedition and had a life-long interest in the Antarctic and the South Atlantic which inspired many of his students.

I well remember his introductory lecture to my year in which he told us to use all the facilities available to us in Cambridge to the full. If we were just going to come to lectures and keep our heads down working, we might as well be on a correspondence course. He exhorted us to join societies and have a wide variety of interests. In fact his message to us was that we were at Cambridge to widen our horizons, to learn to think for ourselves and be able to discern the wood from the trees. He himself was a man with very wide interests and great ability and resourcefulness.

Another of the lecturers in the Department was Gordon Manley, later to become Professor at Lancaster University. His great interest was the weather and he lectured to us on Meteorology and Climatology, both world-wide studies.

It was wartime and weather forecasts were unknown. Such information would have enabled the Germans to plan their air raids more successfully. However, with the aid of instrument readings taken at the University and with his remarkable 'weather wisdom', Professor Manley would usually start his lectures, whatever the topic for the day might be, with a brief weather synopsis and forecast discussion. A memory comes back of him standing in front of us on a bright sunny day doing just this, and being interrupted by the tremendous noise of the American Flying Fortresses overhead setting out on yet another daylight raid.

Geography as studied at Cambridge was a tremendously wide subject, since it was the study of Man and his Environment. At one time we would be delving into the Magna Carta, or following the voyages of the great explorers. Politics and economics came into our course because geographical facts affect these as well as the course of history. We would find ourselves studying tropical medicine, for disease is so often caused by parasites whose distribution is governed by weather or soil conditions.

At times one felt a jack-of-all-trades, perhaps master of none, but for education in its widest sense the course could have had few equals.

Before winning the scholarships which enabled me to go to Cambridge, I had wanted to join the W.R.N.S. However my Headmistress and parents combined to persuade me to take my chance of a university education first. The war ended whilst I was still a student and as a result I was able to follow the full course uninterrupted. I also had the benefit of the returning students whose courses had been curtailed when they went off on active service. Lectures were never quite the same when they returned. Their wide experience made them question all they were taught and this proved stimulating for lecturers and students alike.

In my final year, as with all students, the great question was what to do next. I had enjoyed my time at Cambridge but rejected the thought of research. I wanted to move on to wider horizons, not to go into more detail on fewer issues. I had specialised in Advanced Physiography and Geodetic and Trigonometrical Surveying. The latter led directly to careers for men—but there were no openings for women. I was indeed given the chance to go on a surveying expedition to Iceland, but as the cook! This was just not on.

I was very interested in Meteorology, but to enter the Air Ministry Meteorological Department, Maths or Physics degrees were required. A career here seemed impossible. Then in March 1947, all University Appointments Boards received a message from the Admiralty stating that they required graduates to train as Meteorological Officers. The tale that was told was that someone in the Admiralty suddenly woke up to the fact that amongst those due for demobilisation by March 1948 were a large number of their Meteorological Officers and it would take about a year to replace them. They were willing to take students with any scientific degree and this included Geography.

As soon as the Appointments Board informed me of all this, my mind was made up. I would after all be able to do something useful in the W.R.N.S. and follow up my interest in Meteorology.

On an early summer's day I went before a rather formidable Board of W.R.N.S. and Naval officers to try to explain why I wanted to become a W.R.N.S. Meteorological Officer. I found to my surprise some scarcely veiled hostility and one question asked has always remained vividly in my mind: 'Why does someone as clever as you wish to join the W.R.N.S.?'

I was rather taken aback as it had not occurred to me that the Senior Service did not require intelligent people. However, once I had embarked on my career I found what I thought to be the answer. The ten of us who had been foisted on the W.R.N.S. along with 16 men who came into the Navy to make up a course of 26, were the very first direct entry W.R.N.S. Officers. Until that moment all W.R.N.S. Officers had come up through the ranks, but the urgency of the need by the Navy for our services had forced the W.R.N.S. into accepting us. We were to realise, in many ways to our cost, when on our course that their acceptance had been very reluctant indeed and not in any way thought through in depth. However, that would make another story.

After qualifying I was sent to R.N.A.S. Saint Merryn in Cornwall, where there were two schools: S.N.A.W. — the School of Naval Air Warfare and A.C.S. — the Aircrewmen's School. The former were experienced pilots who came for further training and whilst I was a Meteorological Officer there, squadrons came to work up before going off to the Korean War. The Aircrewmen's school retrained Telegraphist Air Gunners, Chiefs and Petty Officers, to become Observers and was followed by the Observer's School which trained Midshipmen Observers. As well as doing my share of the briefings watch and watch about with the Senior Meteorological Officer, I was also required to lecture to the Aircrewmen and subsequently to the Midshipmen.

One of my very first Met briefings was at the start of a NATO exercise involving, I think, the Dutch and American Navies, and certainly the RAF. I was rather amused at the presence of the latter because of course I would never have been in a position to brief them if I had had to comply with Air Ministry regulations.

Whilst at Saint Merryn I became engaged to Lieutenant Clifford Gould, who was a Fleet Air Arm Observer instructing the Aircrewmen in navigation and we married in 1950, when he was starting a course in Teacher Training at Saint Mark and Saint John, then in Chelsea, having come out of the Navy that year.

I have written this introduction as a background, so that people who have accused me of being unpatriotic or, as Ned Sherrin ('The Listener', 2 June 1983) has implied, been briefed to do the questioning, will perhaps now see that neither accusation is true. I have not wasted the years between the 1950s and the Falklands. I have brought up a family of four and have always kept abreast of current affairs, have read and listened and looked, and all the time have questioned. The latter indeed is my privilege, and that of all inhabitants of this country, for we are a democracy. When we have leaders who think they are above questioning and we are asked by those in power to accept and not question, we will be moving towards one of the two extremes — Fascism or Communism — and it will be a very sorry day indeed for this country.

Cirencester & Tewkesbury Constituency

After teaching Geography at Putney County (now Mayfield Comprehensive), whilst my husband was at college, and then moving around as most young couples do at the start of their married life, we came to Cirencester. Here my husband taught at Powells School and later became head of Stratton Primary School also in the urban district. Three of our four children were born here, the oldest being a year old when we came, and they have all grown up in this delightful area.

We live in the Cirencester and Tewkesbury Constituency and for many years now our Member of Parliament has been Mr Nicholas Ridley. When Mrs Thatcher became Prime Minister in 1979 she appointed Mr Ridley as one of the Ministers of State in the Foreign and Commonwealth Office.

I had corresponded with Mr Ridley on several occasions on local educational matters and to do with a link road after the building of a by-pass. I had also met him once. This came about during a previous election campaign in 1974. A member of the Conservative party was duly knocking on all doors in Queen Elizabeth Road and on coming to mine assumed I would be voting for Mr Ridley. When I very politely asked her a question on Conservative Party Policy she appeared confused and said I must ask Mr Ridley himself. Since I was quite prepared to do this, and during this particular election campaign he was proposing to do a walkabout, it was arranged that he should come to my house when he visited our area.

Thus, one very hot day when we were having tea in the garden with friends, there was a general hubbub in the road and along came the Conservative candidate and his entourage and he duly came down the garden path as I was emerging from the back door. We had quite a lengthy discussion, part of which I remember was about Enoch Powell and immigration. After about five minutes a young secretarial type came down the path, possibly an arranged rescue attempt after a pre-arranged time limit, I felt. However, to her obvious surprise, she was rather curtly told not to interrupt and the discussion continued. During the conversation I did question the value to the Conservative Party of ladies knocking on doors who were not prepared to answer questions—or perhaps were not capable of doing so? Perhaps they were conservative by instinct and not by reason?

When the 1979 election was called I was interested in the controversy raging then about our contribution to the Common Market. Figures had been disclosed which appeared to point to the fact that we were paying more than most other members. On Friday, 13 April it was reported in the *Wilts and Glos Standard* that Mrs Joy Ramsey, Chairman of the Cirencester Conservative Branch, introduced Sir Guy Millard—the new Sub-Area 3 chairman—at a meeting on 19 March. 'Sir Guy said that Mr Callaghan's recent statement in Paris was the beginning of a shameless attempt to put the blame for the Labour Government's economic failure on to the European Community by distorting the facts. It was simply not true that Britain was the largest net contributor ... or likely to be in the future ... on present trends it seemed likely that our net contribution would be less than half of Germany by 1980.'

One afternoon I noticed a lady, clad in pale pink, proceeding from door to door down the opposite side of the road. She appeared to me to be a typical Conservative Party member engaged on house-to-house visits in support of Mr

Cirencester and Tewkesbury Constituency

Ridley and I thought I would ask her views on the level of our payments to the Common Market. Quite some time later in the afternoon the bell rang and I found the pink-clad lady on the doorstep. After brief preliminaries I started to ask my question, but never completed it. To my surprise she looked at me with horror, glanced desperately around to find a number plate, asked if this was Number Eleven, and when I said it was she muttered that she was not supposed to call at this number and scurried hurriedly up the path. I was reminded of the White (though pink) Rabbit and could almost hear her muttering 'Oh, my ears and whiskers!' I'm afraid I found it very difficult not to burst out laughing. I had not realised that I could strike such terror into anyone.

I soon realised that in going down one side of the road, inevitably she had then come up my side. Unfortunately for her she had not taken into account a quirk of the local council. There are very few number thirteens in the whole of Cirencester. Queen Elizabeth Road was no exception and so she had come from number fifteen next door into number eleven—more to be dreaded apparently in this case than number thirteen!

I have always taken an interest in the part Mr Ridley plays in Parliament as I think constituents should know what their parliamentary representative does in their name. Therefore I was very interested when the Government posts were announced by the new Prime Minister, Mrs Thatcher, to discover that Mr Ridley was to be one of the Ministers of State at the Foreign and Commonwealth Office which was headed by Lord Carrington. He was in fact to be responsible for matters relating to Argentina and the Falkland Islands. I well remember the reports of the debate in Parliament in December 1980 when Mr Ridley put forward plans for lease-back and was howled down by members from all parties.

1982

Remembering the early months of 1982, I am not relying on hindsight or claiming any extra knowledge or insight into the course of events, I do indeed remember feeling, along with many others, that we were giving Argentina all the wrong signals. I felt then that the only way to describe Mrs Thatcher's attitude was as one of 'blinkered intransigence'. She appeared to be so obsessed with reducing the rate of inflation that all the consequences of such an obsession apparently did not matter. To have one target in view and to claim the kudos for succeeding in reaching it, without at the same time admitting any responsibility for the side effects seems to me to be the ultimate in self delusion. Her insistence on cuts was directly responsible for the refusal to delay the proposed recall of HMS *Endurance*, this to save what is now a derisory three and a half million pounds! Also the financial cuts were responsible for the British Antarctic Survey threatening to close its base at Grytviken in South Georgia. Concurrently the Government was taking the decision during the debate on the British Nationality Bill, to refuse to grant British citizenship to the Falkland Islanders. All this was reported in the press and on radio and television news and many people were anxious about the impressions that the Government was giving. For example, Mrs Madge Nichols of the Beaconsfield Conservative Association questioned the Prime Minister regarding the proposed withdrawal of HMS *Endurance* and received the reply 'our judgement is that the presence of the Royal Marine Garrison, which unlike HMS *Endurance* is permanently stationed in the Falklands, is sufficient deterrent against any possible aggression.'

Therefore the message went out loud and clear to the Argentinians that as winter approached, HMS *Endurance* would be recalled and that forty-two Royal Marines were the sum total of our defence force. Mr (now Sir) John Nott, the Secretary of State for Defence, insisted on sticking to the cuts in defence spending and showed the world what a low priority the South Atlantic had in the commitments of the Thatcher Government.

The Task Force

Argentina invaded the Falklands on Friday, 2 April. They had taken the law into their own hands, resorted to force and for this they should be condemned. After various conflicting announcements the news of the invasion was confirmed by the Government.

The next day the debate in Parliament was broadcast live and the nation listened to the House agree to support the despatch of the Task Force which had been announced by the Prime Minister. I sat glued to the radio hearing indeed 'the hounds of war' being unleashed; waiting desperately for a voice of reason to be raised; wondering how the Government could possibly justify such a complete *volte-face*. Those islands, so long neglected, so unworthy of defence spending were now to be the cause of enormous expenditure and loss of life. Great sacrifices were to be made in the name of patriotism. We would show the world that we were still a power to be reckoned with.

One voice at last was heard, that of Mr Raymond Whitney, the member of Parliament for Wycombe. He spoke of negotiations that had gone on in the past in particular those between 1970 and 1972, referring to the opening up of links with the Argentine in terms of travel, medical cover, educational and postal facilities and holidays. He asked if we were ready to accept all the implications involved in landing on the islands and pursuing a blockade, including an air blockade. Were we ready to maintain at 8,000 miles distance the scale of military operation involved 200 to 300 miles from the Argentine mainland? He asked that we should not get led astray so that we would lose the whole possibility of negotiating a peaceful settlement. He was roundly accused of defeatism and the Foreign Office was attacked for wanting to be rid of what they regarded as a tiresome problem. He in fact spoke from extensive personal knowledge and experience, as prior to becoming an M.P. he had been a senior diplomat at the British Embassy in Buenos Aires for the years from 1969.

I felt physically sick and could not really believe that in 1982 our reactions would be so predictable. I kept thinking of the Kurt Jooss ballet, *The Green Table*, with its portrayal of the politicians arguing, then war and death and disease stalking abroad, and its final scene with the politicians still arguing around the green table. For this was what would inevitably happen. Whatever the outcome, if we fought a war, men would be sacrificed, and at the end of it we would be back where we started — the war would solve nothing.

And so we all watched as the Task Force got underway. It was like a war in a goldfish bowl as we saw the troops being transported through Equatorial waters to Ascension Island. As I looked at the television pictures I wondered which of the men would not return, for whom it would be a cruise to death, or which would come back horribly maimed. The attitude of many of the people of this country from that time onwards seemed to me to show symptoms of an inferiority complex on a national scale. We had been warned that Argentina might invade the Falklands to divert attention from the internal problems she was experiencing. What a diversion we now had ourselves from economic gloom on the home front, with lengthening dole queues, increasing numbers of bankruptcies and cut-backs on all services. We were great again! Wave the flags! Nobody was going to twist the British Lion's tail! Don't count the cost or the futility of it all! To do that was to be unpatriotic. People who had never known where the Falkland Islands were, knew nothing of their history, or of the conflicting claims to ownership were now determined that our forces should 'go down there and teach the Argies a lesson'.

My husband, an ex-Fleet Air Arm observer, had great doubts about the wisdom of sending a sea force which would be without adequate air cover to combat land-based aircraft from the Argentinian mainland. It appeared to be flouting all previous wisdom of sea warfare, and sending the ships with their human cargoes into terrifying danger. To me, the lessons of previous wars of the danger of extended supply lines loomed large. And so we watched and waited, the ships sailing South, we prayed in our church at Stratton as did congregations in all churches, that a peaceful solution would be found. We listened to reports from the United Nations and watched as the U.S. Secretary of State Alexander Haig tried to find a plan that both sides could accept.

A surprising number of people asked if my second son, Martin, was involved. They knew he was a navigating officer with P. and O., and of course P. and O. ships and personnel were in the Task Force. I would reply that I was thankful that he was in the Indian Ocean, not the Atlantic and would explain how bitterly I felt about his contemporaries being thrown into such a war. The reaction of my listeners was quite extraordinary. Many said that they felt as I did, but they had not liked to express such feelings. We were continually being told by the press and politicians that we were doing a glorious thing, that anyone found guilty of expressing doubts about the wisdom of the action we were taking was branded as unpatriotic.

War

Reality struck home on May 1st. We learned at home of the bombing of the airstrip at Stanley by a Vulcan flying down from Ascension Island in the early hours. This was followed by a naval bombardment of Stanley airport. The Foreign Secretary, Mr Francis Pym, flew to Washington where he had talks with Mr Alexander Haig, whose peace negotiations appeared to have failed and the United States had come down clearly on Britain's side.

On May 2nd the nuclear submarine HMS *Conqueror* sank the Argentinian cruiser *General Belgrano* with the loss of 368 lives. These were the first major casualties of the war. When this news was given at home we were told that the *Belgrano* was outside the Exclusion Zone. We had created this zone of 200 miles around the Falklands on 7 April and had warned Argentina that any ships venturing inside would be sunk on sight. On 23 April this order had been amended: Argentinian ships outside the zone would be sunk if they constituted a threat to our forces.

Immediately doubts sprang up about the wisdom of the sinking, especially since efforts to reach a peaceful solution were still continuing. Doubts also arose as to what immediate threat to our forces the *Belgrano* posed; doubts which were fuelled by conflicting reports.

Doubts which have never been allayed, and which never will be until all the facts are known. But hundreds of men died and a turning-point appeared to have been reached. This was war and all thoughts of a peaceful solution disappeared. The popular press seemed to glory in the war and perhaps the most glaring example of this occurred when *The Sun* used the screaming headline GOTCHA to announce the sinking of the *Belgrano*.

No one who lived through the campaign or who waited for news at home could doubt the bravery of the British forces. They gave of their utmost at the politicians' behest. Thoughts come to mind of the Crimean War with its distant venue and the blunders of the politicians. The bravery of the men involved in the Battle of Balaclava is immortalised by Alfred Lord Tennyson in 'The Charge of the Light Brigade':

> Their's not to make reply,
> Their's not to reason why,
> Their's but to do and die:
> Into the Valley of Death
> Rode the six hundred.

A similar poem could perhaps be written to immortalise those who fought in the far-off Falkland Islands, 8,000 miles from home.

The war continued and at home we listened to the unemotional tones of the Ministry of Defence spokesman, Ian McDonald, announcing the loss of HMS *Sheffield* on 4 May, the continued bombardment of Stanley, the landings on 21 May with the loss of HMS *Ardent* and *Antelope*, the loss of the *Atlantic Conveyor* and HMS *Coventry* on 25 May. We were paying a high price indeed in ships and men, both at the landings and in the fighting on land where our soldiers were showing great courage and endurance. Finally on 14 June the Argentine forces surrendered and then came the reckoning. And what a cost it was to prove in ships and aircraft and, above all, in men's lives, so that 1,800 men, women and children could continue to live under the Union Jack. Do they really feel that the sacrifice made by others for them was justified? And that more and more sacrifices will have to be made in order to preserve the *status quo*?

The Aftermath

At home each returning ship was given a great welcome, with the exception of HMS *Endurance*, and honours were bestowed and flags were waved. A service of thanksgiving was arranged. This led to recriminations. Mrs Thatcher wished it to be a paean of triumph; the Archbishop on the other hand had more Christian views and remembered the dead of both countries.

The Franks Committee set to work under the chairmanship of Lord Franks to prepare the Falkland Islands Review, which was duly presented to Parliament by the Prime Minister in January 1983. Its purpose was 'to review the way in which the responsibilities of Government in relation to the Falkland Islands and their Dependencies were discharged in the period leading up to the Argentinian invasion of the Falkland Islands on 2nd April 1982, taking account of such factors in the previous years as are relevant'. It was not a report into the conduct of the war, and therefore such disasters as Bluff Cove and the sinking of the *Belgrano* were in no way to be investigated or reported on. Surprisingly many people concerned with news distribution seem to imply that the Report covered the whole of the war.

In order to make a reasoned judgement of what happened in April 1982 it is obviously necessary to study the events of previous years as done by the Franks Committee. Therefore, information obtained from the Report is included here.

Part II
The Franks Report

1965-1979

The Report itself makes interesting reading even though the conclusions seem somewhat surprising. It begins with the Resolution passed at the United Nations Assembly in December 1965 about bringing to an end everywhere colonialism in all its forms, and called on the United Kingdom and Argentina to proceed without delay with negotiations with a view to finding a peaceful solution to the problem of the Falkland Islands (Malvinas).

It follows through with the negotiations that took place between the two countries. The Argentinians would not negotiate without the question of sovereignty being discussed. We refused to do this. Argentina went back to the United Nations and in 1974 a resolution by the General Assembly called on both parties to accelerate negotiations towards a solution of the sovereignty case.

Pressure mounted in Argentina in spite of commercial agreements being made, and in April 1975 our new Ambassador delivered a warning that an attack on the Islands would meet with military response. In July of that year, following a proposal by the Defence Committee for joint Anglo Argentine development of the resources of the South West Atlantic, their Minister for Foreign Affairs suggested linking this initiative to the possibility of a transfer of sovereignty followed by simultaneous lease-back for a period of years as a means of settling the dispute. At the same time Argentina proposed that they should occupy the uninhabited islands of South Georgia and the South Sandwich Islands. Again talks broke down and tension mounted. The Joint Intelligence Committee warned that a deliberately planned invasion could not be wholly excluded.

In spite of the circumstances in the South-West Atlantic the 1974 Defence Review which was concerned with the run-down of commitments outside of NATO, decided to take HMS *Endurance*, which patrolled during the summer months, out of service. However it was retained on an annual basis until 1978, and then the Secretary of State for Defence, Fred Mulley, agreed to two further deployments, 1979/80 and 1980/81. In February 1976 Mr Callaghan called for discussion in the Defence Committee and the Chiefs of Staff submitted a paper which showed very clearly all the problems that would be involved in just such an operation as did take place in 1982. Therefore, in March 1976 Mr Callaghan decided to undertake a major review of policy and negotiations were to be resumed, including the discussion of sovereignty. At about the same time in Argentina, as the result of a coup, the military Junta came to power.

Again in December 1976 the UN General Assembly passed a resolution to expedite negotiations. Our Intelligence indicated that there had been a contingency for invasion of the Falklands combined with the diplomatic initiative at the UN and in fact an Argentine military presence had been discovered on Southern Thule in the South Sandwich Islands in December 1976 by an *Endurance* helicopter.

In February 1977 the Foreign Secretary, Mr Crosland, announced we would resume negotiations but that the Government would reserve their position on sovereignty and the islanders were to be fully consulted. At the same time the Government rejected much of the long-term economic survey undertaken by Lord Shackleton (published May 1976) as far too costly. By July 1977 Dr David Owen was the Foreign Secretary and he presented a paper to the Defence Committee stating that serious negotiations were necessary because the Islands were militarily indefensible except by an enormously costly and unacceptable diversion of current resources. He favoured a lease-back solution with time to educate public opinion at home and in the Islands, and proposed that sovereignty of the uninhabited Dependencies might be looked at separately from sovereignty of the Falkland Islands themselves. However, when talks did take place later that year lease-back was not proposed.

Before the end of the year, because of failures in disputes with Brazil and Chile, it was felt that the Junta's attitude was hardening on the Falklands problem. Once again the Joint Intelligence Committee warned that invasion could not be discounted. Because of the deteriorating situation the Chiefs of Staff were called on, as in February 1976, and the same conclusions on the difficulties and costs of combatting an invasion were reached. And so by the time there was a change of government in 1979 there had been a long period of abortive negotiations, warnings of invasion and less and less room for manoeuvre because of the attitude of the islanders.

1979-1982

The incoming occupants of the Foreign Office found the problem waiting for them. It just would not go away, and never will. According to Franks the options were: 1. Fortress Falklands; 2. Give up the Islands and resettle the islanders; 3. Pretend to negotiate, or 4. Negotiate in good faith. Option two was rejected as politically and morally indefensible, but could surely have been combined with option four. Reading the Report it appears to me that there were really only two options. Option One, spend a great deal of money on the Islands to develop them and of necessity to protect them, that is Fortress Falklands, or Option Two, negotiate in good faith, which would mean the transfer of sovereignty because Argentina would not negotiate without this. Surely one side cannot negotiate on its own! In order to comply with the islanders' wishes to maintain their way of life and not live under a dictatorship, some resettlement scheme would have had to be offered them under the second option. Such a scheme was the solution that many of those against fighting a war were hoping would be put forward in a negotiated peace, with realistic compensation being paid to the islanders. Fighting the war appeared to lead inevitably to Option One, Fortress Falklands.

In the event, the Foreign Office embarked on Option Four, that is, to negotiate in good faith, but from the

Report the negotiations appear to have deteriorated into Option Three, a playing for time. Apparently when Mr Nicholas Ridley went to the Falkland Islands in July 1979 the councillors wanted to 'freeze' the dispute. In view of all that had gone before, how could they imagine that a freeze on our side could do other than hot up the other side? By doing nothing and adopting an ostrich-like posture we would have taken the certain path to provocation.

Those outside the Foreign Office appear to accuse the FO of constantly stirring up trouble, wanting to get rid of the Islands. I am sure that anyone who found themselves appointed to that office, whatever their views might have been before, would quickly have discovered that the problem was such that something had to be done and that the islanders could not just be left in blissful somnolence.

Lord Carrington, Secretary of State for Foreign and Commonwealth Affairs, put forward three options in September 1979: 1. Fortress Falklands; 2. Protracted negotiations with no concession on sovereignty, and 3. Substantive negotiations on sovereignty. He advocated the last and suggested lease-back. The Prime Minister, Mrs Thatcher, however, would not agree. Thus, in October 1979 he circulated a memorandum to the Prime Minister and Defence Committee stating that following Options One and Two carried a serious threat of invasion and that the Argentinians were quite capable of capturing the Islands. Mrs Thatcher decided that the Defence Committee should postpone discussion. In November 1979 the Joint Intelligence Committee, though hedging somewhat did say that if negotiations broke down there was a high risk of the Argentinians resorting to force.

In January 1980 the Defence Committee invited Lord Carrington to seek written confirmation from the Falkland Islands Council that it wished talks to be resumed with the Argentine Government, and to propose new terms of reference for them. This was done and talks were held in New York in April 1980, led by Mr Nicholas Ridley and an Island councillor participated.

In July 1980 the Defence Committee agreed to attempt a solution, on the basis of a leaseback agreement, and following a November meeting Mr Ridley was sent again to the Islands to assess the level of support, which turned out to be divided. Then followed the very hostile reaction in the Commons when Mr Ridley presented his statement in December of that year.

Following a Defence Committee review in January 1981, Mr Ridley proposed a 'freeze' of the dispute, as requested by the islanders. Not surprisingly, this was rejected outright by the Argentinians. Thus, in March Lord Carrington told Mrs Thatcher and the Defence Committee that if the islanders preferred the status quo, it would be necessary to prepare for the possibility of a deterioration of relations with Argentina which might involve supplying the islanders if Argentina withdrew her services, and perhaps defending them against physical harassment. In May the British Ambassador in Buenos Aires wrote to the Foreign Office urging more talks. The Foreign Office replied that it was 'under no illusions about the limits of Argentinian patience or risk of serious confrontation'. At the end of June, at a meeting in Mr Ridley's office, at which the Falkland Islands Governor and the Ambassador to Argentina were present, it was stressed that there was a need to educate islander and UK opinion about the danger of inaction. A number of measures were suggested, including a resettlement scheme. It also recommended that if nothing were offered to Argentina, consideration should be given to preparing fuller contingency plans for the defence and development of the Islands. The Ambassador had earlier indicated that islander opinion of the realities had been allowed to slide back. He also wanted to bring home to British public opinion the potential cost of any alternative to a peaceful solution, and he warned of the risk of Argentina using Britain as a scapegoat for its domestic troubles. However, the Governor reported that the islanders wished to have nothing to do with the Argentinians. It was obviously becoming a question of playing for time.

In July 1981 the Joint Intelligence Committee expressed the view that there might be disruption of air and sea communications. The Argentinians might occupy one of the island dependencies as they had done in 1976 and there was a risk that they might establish a military presence in the Falklands themselves, though possibly remote from Port Stanley. In fact its report concluded that if Argentina decided there was no hope of a peaceful transfer of sovereignty, there was a high risk of them resorting to more forcible measures, that they might act swiftly and without warning, and full invasion could not be discounted.

Mr Ridley in his report to Lord Carrington warned that if Argentina concluded—possibly by early 1982—that there would be no negotiations, then 'serious retaliatory action must be expected'. He also wanted contingency action to deal with the consequences.

In September 1981 a minute was sent to Mrs Thatcher and the members of the Defence Committee, but a meeting was not called for.

The British Ambassador in Buenos Aires was moved to protest strongly in a letter that inaction after the advice given at the June meeting in Mr Ridley's office, meant the islanders would never accept sovereignty transfer. He indeed wrote that if it was not possible to negotiate then Britain should say so frankly and face the consequences.

In the meantime, early in June Lord Carrington had written to Mr John Nott, Secretary of State for Defence, urging him to retain HMS *Endurance*, due to be withdrawn in March 1982, as such a withdrawal would be interpreted as a reduction of commitment and willingness to defend the Islands. However, the decision to withdraw *Endurance* was confirmed in Parliament at the end of that month. Argentine newspapers immediately highlighted the theme of our abandonment of protection of the Falklands. Further pressure was put on Mr Nott in January 1982 and on 3 February he replied to it by declining to reverse his decision.

Whilst these decisions were being taken by our Government, the end of December 1981 had seen General Galtieri become President of Argentina and Dr Costa Mendez take over again as Foreign Minister, a post he had held in the late 1960s. The view expressed at our Foreign Office was that a more forceful approach could now be expected.

The Governor of the Falkland Islands in his review of 1981, which was submitted in January 1982, showed clearly the deterioration in the islanders' relations with both Britain and Argentina and that their suspicions of the Government's intentions had been increased by its refusal to grant British citizenship to the Falkland Islands in the British Nationality Bill, by announcing the withdrawal of HMS *Endurance* and by financial cuts in the British Antarctic Survey, especially the threatened closure of its base at Grytviken in South Georgia. There appeared to be no way ahead as long as the Argentine insisted on sovereignty first and the British continued to maintain that the islanders' wishes were paramount.

The islanders had received clear 'signals' that Mrs Thatcher's Government was more interested in making cuts in public spending than spending money to protect them. It is therefore not unreasonable to suppose that Argentina received the same signals. An analysis of the Governor's report spoke of the dispute moving sooner or later to more open confrontation and a formal reply in March to the Governor pointed out the difficulties for the Government of finding the necessary finance to replace the services and to defend the Islands. It stated that unless a negotiated settlement could be reached the way forward for the islanders could only be downhill.

Further talks began in New York at the end of February and Lord Carrington sent a minute to Mrs Thatcher before these in which he suggested the Defence Committee would be expected to discuss the Falklands in March. In reply Mrs Thatcher commented that it must be made clear to the Argentines that the wishes of the islanders were paramount. The Argentine press went to town on reports of the New York meeting and it was after a telegram from the British Ambassador in Buenos Aires on 3 March that Mrs Thatcher wrote on it 'we must make contingency plans', and on 8

March she was advised by Mr Nott that it would take twenty days to deploy Royal Navy ships to the Falkland Islands if they were required.

Taking place concurrently with the diplomatic moves at this crucial time, late 1981 and early 1982, were the 'scrap metal' landings on South Georgia and Captain Barker of HMS *Endurance* was also reporting Argentinian Air Force activity over that island. As late as 24 March, in a minute to Mrs Thatcher and other members of the Defence Committee, Lord Carrington recommended an early meeting of the Committee and sought approval to meet the costs of a suggested replacement of sea and air services to the Falklands from the Contingency Reserve. This was refused by the Treasury on 29 March. Also on 24 March Lord Carrington again sought agreement from Mr Nott for HMS *Endurance* to stay on station and this was agreed on 26 March.

Intense naval activity was reported in Argentinian ports on 27 March, but this could have been explained as part of a joint Argentine-Uruguayan anti-submarine exercise then in progress. However, the Royal Fleet Auxiliary *Fort Austin* was ordered from Gibraltar on 29 March and a nuclear submarine was dispatched and a second one followed the next day. Mr Nott was given intelligence on 31 March that Argentina might invade the Falklands early on 2 April and the Naval Staff were instructed to prepare a Task Force.

At last, on 1 April, the Defence Committee did discuss the Falkland Islands problem. It is astonishing that this was the first time it had been formally discussed outside the Foreign and Commonwealth Office since January 1981.

By midday on 2 April Argentinian landings on the Falklands were confirmed and at 7.30 p.m. the Cabinet met and agreed that the Task Force should be despatched and the emergency debate in the House of Commons followed on Saturday, 3 April.

The Task Force departed, Lord Carrington and Mr Luce resigned. Later Mr Nott was to resign. Therefore, those who advised the Prime Minister and to whom she turned a deaf ear, all left the Government. The one person in charge of the whole situation, Mrs Thatcher, remained and gained enormous public acclaim. The conclusions that the Franks Report came to in the light of all the evidence given seem extraordinary: 'we conclude that we would not be justified in attaching any criticism or blame to the present Government for the Argentine Junta's decision to commit its act of unprovoked aggression in the invasion of the Falkland Islands on 2nd April 1982'.

Part III
1983 Election Year

Cotswold Town and Country

The Franks Report and subsequent debates in the House and the press reports and the publication of several Falkland books kept the issue of the war well to the forefront throughout the spring of 1983.

Early in April a free newspaper, subsidised by advertisements, came through our letterbox. It was the monthly news magazine called 'Cotswold Town and Country', published in Wotton-under-Edge and with editorial offices in Malmesbury. Its editorial is so biased towards the Conservatives that I regard it as party political propaganda and usually consign it straight into the waste bin.

On this occasion, however, I turned to page 2 and found the paper's editor attacking a letter that he did not agree with. This seems to be the usual practice and possibly the paper only publishes such letters to use as a springboard. Along with the letter commenting on Mr Ridley's attack on CND was another one headed 'T.V. distortion', and the words 'General Belgrano' caught my eye, so I read on. It was a complaint by Eric Alderson of Cirencester about T.V. reports during the Falklands war. He said that he had felt distressed about the sinking of the Argentinian cruiser when she was apparently steaming away from our Task Force and on her way to base. He continued, 'I now learn from Intelligence reports that this ship was at the centre of a battle group converging on the British Task Force and

Cotswold Town and Country 45

not heading in a south-westerly direction as we were informed by the BBC (who apparently preferred the Argentine version of the sinking)'.

I wondered what Intelligence reports he had access to in April 1983 which appeared to contradict all that I had previously read about the sinking. I immediately looked in the telephone directory, but could find no phone number, so I was unable to ask him about his source. I then threw away the paper, but somehow could not forget the letter.

A few days later an article in *The Guardian* referred to Mr Tam Dalyell, M.P., and this reminded me of his great interest in the sinking of the *Belgrano* and I decided on the spur of the moment to write and ask him about this latest 'intelligence'. I retrieved the newspaper from the kitchen waste bin and cut out the relevant portion and sent it to him with apologies for the state it was in. I explained why it was not as clean as it might have been and asked him to comment on the letter. I received a reply from him from Linlithgow, dated 24 April. In it he told me that the Government's own replies said there was no unit of the Task Force West of the *Belgrano*, the direction in which she was steaming and he referred me to *Hansard*, 21 December 1982 and 24 March 1983, which he thought I would be able to find in the local library.

'Hansard'

A visit to the Bingham Library proved fruitless, no *Hansards* were kept there. However, I was given a pamphlet with information about the reference section of the Cheltenham Public Library and told that they would supply photocopies at a reasonable price. Back home again I rang the number given and expalined what I wanted. 'Yes, they did keep copies of *Hansard*. Yes, I could have photocopies at a cost of 10p. a sheet. Exactly which sheets did I want?'

    I gave the two dates and said that I had no idea how many pages might be involved, but that I wanted any references to the sinking of the *Belgrano*. The librarian suggested that they would look up the two dates and go through them quickly to see how many sheets were needed. She herself was going off duty, but she would pass on the message to a colleague who would ring me back later. An hour or so later the phone rang and I was given the information that thirteen sheets appeared to cover my requirements and it was arranged that these should be photocopied and posted to me. The matter was dealt with so helpfully and promptly that when I sent my cheque off to Miss Shipway, whose name appeared on the covering letter, I expressed my grateful thanks.

    I then started to read the pages and on the very first one, column 897 of 21 December 1982, Falklands Campaign, where Mr Tam Dalyell was seeking an enquiry into the circumstances surrounding the decision to sink the *General Belgrano*, I read the following:

> By parliamentary question it has been established that when the *General Belgrano* was torpedoed, her position was 55 degrees 27 minutes south, 61 degrees 25 minutes west. By parliamentary question it has been established that she was on a course of 280 degrees, that is on course for the Straits of Magellan and her home port of Uschaia in the Southern Argentine. By parliamentary question it has been established that there were no units of the task force west of the *General Belgrano*. Indeed, in answer to question No 102 on 16 December the Prime Minister said:

> 'The vessels of the Task Force were, broadly speaking, to the north-east . . .' (Official Report, 16 December 1982; Volume 34, c. 201)

> How are we to explain the following statement from the Secretary of State for Defence:

> 'This heavily armed surface attack group was close to the total exclusion zone and was closing on elements of our Task Force which was only hours away' (Official Report, 4 May 1982; Volume 23, c. 29-30)

I wondered yet again what Intelligence reports Mr Eric Alderson had access to which had not been made available to Parliament. I plotted the position of the *Belgrano* on a map, drew in the exclusion zone and noted where the shallower waters were. Part of these must have been the Burdwood Bank which was referred to in the Official Report, 29 November 1982, Volume 33, c. 104, which said:

> Concerned that HMS *Conqueror* might lose the *General Belgrano* as she ran over the shallow water of the Burdwood Bank, the Task Force commander sought and obtained a change in the rules of engagement to allow an attack outside the 200-mile exclusion zone.

Mr Tam Dalyell pointed out that the *Belgrano* was at least

45 miles to the south-west of the edge of the Burdwood Bank and was heading west-north-west and he therefore wanted to know what positive evidence was available at the time she was torpedoed that the *Belgrano* would change her course and head for the Burdwood Bank, and the reply was:

> It would not be in the public interest to go into details. (Official Report, 14 December 1982; Volume 34, c. 59)

He had already established that there was 25 fathoms (150 feet) of water in the shallowest part of the Burdwood Bank, and that the *Conqueror* was of the Valiant class of submarine equipped with sonar that allows them to operate in the shallow Baltic Sea. It therefore appears that the fears of the Task Force commander, Sir Sandy Woodward, were not very well founded. Other discrepancies occur in the early reports. The White Paper states 'on 2 May HMS *Conqueror* detected the Argentine cruiser *General Belgrano*'. Later some members of the crew were to state that HMS *Conqueror* detected the *Belgrano* and her escorts the *Piedra Buena* and the *Hipolito Bouchard* at least 24 hours before she was sunk at 1457 hours, South Atlantic time, which would mean she was sighted on 1 May.

Again the Secretary of State for Defence said:

> The actual decision to launch a torpedo was clearly one taken by the submarine commander. (Official Report, 5 May 1982; Volume 23, c. 156)

Later Commander Wreford-Brown of the *Conqueror* stated that his orders to sink the *Belgrano* had come from Northwood.

Mr Tam Dalyell referred to the serious peace proposals emanating from the United States and Peru that were reaching the Prime Minister on the morning of 2 May.

Mr Nott, the Defence Secretary, interrupted him to say that a large proportion of the charges made were completely untrue, but left everyone in doubt as to which he referred to. He had just announced his resignation after 15 years and in spite of the reasons given, left many people wondering if they had heard all of them.

An Election is Called

Not long after I had acquired my copies of *Hansard*, BBC Television produced a documentary-type programme on the Peruvian Peace Plan which I watched with great interest. The programme appeared to suggest that the plan was thought out on the evening of 1 May and that it was virtually ready for signing when the news came through of the sinking of the *Belgrano* and all hopes of peace were scuppered. This certainly seemed to confirm Mr Tam Dalyell's statement in the House on 21 December 1982 and his repeated accusations, as recorded in *Hansard* on 24 March 1983.

We were now living through the weeks of 'Maggie May — or Maggie May Not'. Would the Prime Minister go to the country after only four of her possible five years in office? Would she stay longer? Why, if all her policies were going to plan, would she feel it necessary to cut and run, especially with a summit at both Stuttgart and in America in the offing? In the event she decided to go to the country.

In the House on 12 May, in what appeared to be an unguarded moment, Mrs Thatcher stated vehemently that she had not known of the Peace Plan when the *Belgrano* was sunk. I heard this on the radio and was stunned! Could it possibly be true? If so, what had happened to our communications system? I reread the debates in *Hansard* and there Mr Tam Dalyell said:

50 An Election is Called

> No one has yet dented my account of the inter-locking between the Peruvian Peace Plan and sinking of the *Belgrano*. (24 March 1983)

How strange it seemed to me that Mrs Thatcher's words were spoken when Parliament was being disbanded, and that such a statement had not been made to refute Mr Dalyell's claim on 24 March. Did she do this deliberately, so that she could not be questioned further for some time? Did she speak without thinking, letting a very strange 'cat out of a bag'? Was it the absolute truth? Had I even heard it correctly?

Apparently that evening during the adjournment debate, Mr Tam Dalyell repeated his allegations, accusing Mrs Thatcher yet again of ordering the sinking of the *Belgrano* to wreck the peace proposal put forward by the President of Peru. In denying the charge the Foreign Office minister, Mr Cranley Onslow, stated that the *Belgrano* was attacked because it posed a threat to ships of the Task Force and confirmed Mrs Thatcher's statement by saying that the Peruvian proposals reached London after the attack.

It was probably on 13 May that a television news reader, in repeating Mr Cranley Onslow's confirmation, appeared to break off from reading the news to comment that this threw a new light on the programme about the Peruvian Peace Plan, and suggested that perhaps there should be an enquiry. Thus it was on 13 May that I learned of his confirmation.

The Letter

I could not reconcile what I felt were the facts about the events which occurred on 1st and 2nd May 1982, and this latest disclosure by Mrs Thatcher, I could not get out of my mind.

One evening my husband said that they were asking for questions on 'Nationwide', so why not write it all down? He had been watching television and had heard of the proposed programmes for questioning the leaders of the political parties in the run-up to the election. He knew that the 'On The Spot' programmes meant direct confrontation, but somehow this did not come across to me — I did not even know the title. I was still thinking of the news reader's remarks about an enquiry. I felt I could contribute towards it and that I would get rid of what was becoming an obsession. I thought they might incorporate my ideas in their programme but was totally unaware of the need to appear on the programme. It had never been an ambition of mine to appear on the 'box' and possibly had I known more about the programme I would never have written as I did.

On 16 May I sat down with my atlas in front of me and wrote my letter, which I headed 'The Lost Hours':

Having studied *Hansard* for the 21st December 1982 and the 24th March 1983 and watched the television programme about the peace initiative by Peru, I was astounded when Mrs Thatcher declared in Parliament on 12th May that she did not get news of the Peace Plan proposals until late on 2nd May after the *Belgrano* was sunk. This was repeated on May 13th by Mr Cranley Onslow.

Surely an enquiry must be made in order to discover how such a disastrous delay in communications at top levels, at so critical a time, could occur?

Peru is bisected by the 75° West longitude which would appear to put it in the same time zone as New York. Therefore if the Peace Plan was formulated in Peru on the evening of 1st May, at midnight there, it would have been midnight in New York and 0500 G.M.T. on May 2nd in London. There is therefore a gap of seven hours i.e. 0500 G.M.T. to 1200 G.M.T. (1300 B.S.T.) when Peru and presumably the United States and therefore feasibly Mr Francis Pym, the Foreign Secretary, in New York should have known of the Peace Plan and could have transmitted it to London before Mrs Thatcher made her pre-lunch decision at Chequers on May 2nd.

The *Belgrano* was sunk at 1457 hours South Atlantic Time at longitude 61° 25m West which means that in London it was about 1900 G.M.T. (2000 B.S.T.) and 1400 hours in New York and Peru. This means that there were a further seven hours from 1200 G.M.T. (1300 B.S.T.) — lunch time at Chequers — until 1900 G.M.T. (2000 B.S.T.) when the *Belgrano* was sunk, in which, in the light of the Peace Proposals, the order to the *Conqueror* could have been rescinded. This makes a grand total of 14 hours from midnight on May 1st in Peru during which the Prime Minister and her Cabinet were apparently kept in ignorance of the Peace Proposals.

The question is therefore why was there this fourteen-hour delay, with all such a delay implies about our lack of intelligence information and communications and Mr Francis Pym's failure to communicate with the Prime

The Letter

Minister when he was with the Americans in New York?

The next day I went into the General Post Office and tried to find an address for 'Nationwide'. I decided that the B.B.C. News Studio at Lime Grove would probably ensure that my letter reached its destination and so I posted it on 17 May.

In writing the letter I had made several assumptions. I did not know, for example, whether New York or Peru indulged in Summer Time as we do here. I also decided that the evening of 1 May should extend up to midnight, although I realised that talks could have gone on later than this. I also decided that one o'clock was a reasonable time for Mrs Thatcher to have her lunch at Chequers. Allowing for the fact that all these assumptions might not be completely accurate there were still an awful lot of 'Lost Hours'.

Two days later I received the phone call from 'Nationwide' and had to make the decision whether to appear on the programme. I explained to Julie that I would be out next day until teatime as I was invigilating C.S.E. examinations at Cirencester School. She said she would ring me back in the early evening. When she got through again she told me that they definitely wanted me to put my question to Mrs Thatcher and we both felt that a preliminary question about the actual sinking would set the scene. I agreed that I would appear and said I would be free from 12.30 p.m. on Tuesday, 24th. She told me to expect a phone call from Bristol at about 5 p.m. on Monday when I would be home from school, to arrange about transport.

On Monday morning I decided I really ought to know exactly what I had let myself in for and so I called in to Baily and Woods, an old Cirencester newsagents, to find out if they still had a copy of the current *Radio Times*. They did, and so I bought it and turned to the page for Tuesday's programmes. There I found a photograph of Mrs Thatcher and the heading 'Nationwide and Election 83. Mrs Thatcher On The Spot'. So now I knew!

I made sure I was at home by 5 p.m., but no phone call came. I decided that the presenters had changed their minds and did not need my contribution. I had not told anyone outside the family about the programme because I did not want to be drawn into any arguments or discussions. Even members of the family would only know by post on the morning of the 24th. Like many people I was not worried about what strangers and the general public might think of me, but felt very self conscious at appearing before family and friends.

Eventually, well after 7 p.m. the phone call came. Bob Lynton from the B.B.C. Television Studios, Bristol, arranged that a taxi would pick me up from Cirencester School at 12.30 p.m. and take me to the studios in Whiteladies Road in time to have lunch. He gave me a number to ring by 12.45 in case the taxi did not turn up. When I asked what would happen then, he—jokingly, I am sure—said he would send a helicopter! This was not so difficult to imagine actually, since Colt Car Company regularly uses a field near the school as a helicopter terminal.

May 24th 1983

All Tuesday morning I tried to keep my attention on the youngsters sitting their exams, but my imagination was running riot. What would the studios be like, was I really going to be on the programme, couldn't I just quietly forget about it? Inevitably 12.30 came round, however, and so, very promptly, did the taxi, to the Administrative Office of the School. I saw it arrive and went out immediately and departed without anyone at the school being any the wiser.

We were at the Studios just before 1.30 p.m. and after waiting for some more arrivals Bob Lynton escorted us into the canteen for lunch. Needless to say we discussed the programme whilst eating and were surprised to discover the number of potential questions that 'Nationwide' had lined up. I believe five centres were involved in the link-up and each centre was providing four candidates, making a total of twenty questions in all. Since the programme was only from 6.25 to 7.00 p.m. we all felt that some or all of us would not be called upon and tried to ascertain whether it would be a case of asking a question and then meekly listening to an answer, or whether, as we all wished, we would be able to follow up the answer.

After lunch we went into a studio and it was interesting to discover that it was the one from which 'Points West' is broadcast. We sat on four seats facing across the room towards the 'Points West' desk and looking towards several cameras. We were told which camera we were to look at and I was to look at number two. We were also told that we would not be able to see Mrs Thatcher, only to hear her, but I believe she could both see and hear us. I felt that made our task more difficult and jokingly asked if they would put a wig over the top of the camera!

Sue Lawley then spoke to us from London and we briefly gave the gist of what we would say. There was some discussion about whether to read our questions or not. The general feeling was that it would come across more naturally if we could manage without reading but that it would be a good idea to have the questions on cards just in case we dried up. This was what I dreaded would happen to me.

We sat in the order that Sue Lawley was hoping to follow. Defence questions were coming early in the programme, so I sat on the right side of the row, next to a Mr Ken Stanton from Cheltenham whose brief was the National Health Service. Next to him came a pensioner from Weston-Super-Mare and finally at the other end of the row a young man from Taunton who was interested in Law and Order.

After a cup of tea in the canteen we were free for an hour or so before returning to the Studio for our ordeal. It was a pleasant sunny day and we all elected to go out and once outside went our separate ways. I don't know about the others, but I wanted to be able to think a bit more about my question and did not particularly want to be drawn into further discussion. I turned left and went down towards the town whilst the others went right. I knew the area fairly well as I had been born in Bristol, although I left there when I was four. However, I can remember visiting a very elderly relative who lived in Woodlands Road. I have renewed my acquaintance with Bristol from time to time and still have relatives there. I went towards the shops and came to the large store, Dingles. I had decided to go there in order to buy some light grey summer gloves. I needed them to complete my outfit for my elder son's wedding in August. I had tried to

May 24th 1983

buy the gloves locally and in Cheltenham, and discovered that I could have pink, purple, green — in fact any colour it seemed, but not light grey. Dingles, however, obliged. They had just one pair of light grey and they were my size, so whatever else might happen I had made some use of my visit to Bristol!

On the way back to the studios I noticed that suddenly the steps outside the Victoria Rooms were swarming with women and children. It was the start of a Women's Day for Peace demonstration and they went on to 'die' across the main road, disrupting the homeward rush of traffic.

Back in the studio we quietly filed in whilst 'Points West' drew to a close. Sitting there frantically sipping the water thoughtfully provided, as my throat and mouth got drier and drier, I wondered why on earth I had agreed to take part. I felt as I always do when sitting in the dentist's chair: amazed that I had voluntarily put myself in such a position.

The programme started. We heard the youngster from Plymouth — she sounded so confident — then I seemed to hear from a long way off Sue Lawley saying my name. This really was the moment! I heard myself asking the question, but it all seemed so unreal.

'Why, when you knew the *Belgrano* was outside the exclusion zone and was sailing away from the Falklands did you order it to be sunk?'

To my amazement Mrs Thatcher's first sentence was that it was sailing towards the Falklands. She continued about it being a danger to our ships. I was quite certain that when it was sunk it was sailing away from the Falklands. Had I not read it for myself in *Hansard*, and heard it broadcast last year and read about it in the press?

I was urged on by a whisper from Ken Stanton on my left, 'Keep going, you've got her rattled'. This gave me the courage to continue and to point out that when the cruiser was sunk it was well outside and to the west of the Exclusion Zone and sailing on a bearing of 280°, which is slightly north of west and therefore could in no way be described as sailing towards the Exclusion Zone.

Mrs Thatcher then repeated that the *Belgrano* was a danger to our ships, and that her 'duty was to look after our troops, our ships, our Navy and that she had lived with many, many anxious days and nights'. With a helpful prompt from Sue Lawley I was able to bring in what had originally been my main point, about such an action being likely to sabotage any peace plan, and immediately Mrs Thatcher stated that she had not known about the Peruvian Peace Plan when the attack was made and that we would have to wait for thirty years until all the facts could be published.

I did manage to make my final point that I felt there were about 14 hours in which she could have had some information and that as we were living in a nuclear push-button age those in power would have minutes not hours in which to take decisions.

I felt then, and do now, that we should not have to wait for thirty years; that 'important intelligence considerations' make a marvellous screen to hide behind, and that both Mrs Thatcher and I would be in our mid-eighties, or more likely dead, before all the facts would be published.

The programme continued and I subsided back into my chair, still feeling that perhaps I would wake up from a dream, or rather a nightmare! I gradually took in the rest of the questions and noticed that Mrs Thatcher was insisting on having her say and appeared to be over-riding Sue Lawley, so that questions on National Health were curtailed and my 'encourager' did not get a chance to put his own question. Then a pensioner questioned Mrs Thatcher about the fall in value of the Christmas bonus and as time was running out our pensioner from Bristol missed his opportunity. One topic that had not been covered was Law and Order, and so to round off the programme Sue Lawley called on our questioner from Taunton and the programme was over.

Then came a babble of noise as we all started to talk, a relief of tension and an inquest on the programme. The organisers had been able to watch on a screen and described to us Mrs Thatcher's reaction to my questions which appeared to have been quite remarkable. This, of course, was the impression given to many viewers. Whilst we were talking a message was brought in to me asking if I would take a phone call from the *Daily Express*. By this time the relief that the ordeal was over, plus the reactions of people around me, made me feel I could take on the world! What was one *Daily Express* reporter?

I was led to an office and handed the phone. The occupant of the office could only hear my side of the conversation, but I could see he was highly amused. The conversation went roughly like this:

'Is that Miss Diana Gould?'

'No, this is Mrs Diana Gould. I happen to have four children.'

'Oh, you would be about thirty-six or so? . . . from your voice . . . you sound about that.'

'That is very flattering. I happen to be about the same age as Mrs Thatcher. I was at Cambridge when she was at Oxford. But it appears obvious to me that you have neither seen nor heard the programme, so why on earth are you interviewing me?'

'Well, no. I'm sorry about that, but I have had a message from London to try to contact you. Do you come from Bristol?'

'No, I live in Cirencester.' — A longish pause.

'Cirencester? . . . What street?'

'Just Cirencester.' I really did not see why I should disclose my complete address.

'Do you belong to any political party?'

'No and I never have done so, but that does not mean to say that I do not use my vote.'

'Would you mind telling me which party you will be voting for?'

'Well, no . . . as a matter of fact I grew up in a Tory-voting household. But when I went to Cambridge and really began to think for myself — I decided that my sympathies were with the Labour party. I will be voting Labour again this time.'

I think I must have touched him on the raw by castigating him, and therefore his paper, for getting a non-viewer to conduct the enquiry, as he ended up by apologising and saying that the paper 'Did not usually do things this way'.

I understood from a phone call some days later from 'Nationwide' that Mrs Thatcher was very upset indeed with the programme and the presenters, and repeated what she had said to me, that such questioning of a Prime Minister could only happen in a democracy. I still do not know why she felt she had to say this. We are a democracy. We can question. She seemed to be questioning the wisdom of this. Possibly she feels that she should be out of reach of the electorate? But it is the people who put her where she is, and she is ultimately answerable to them.

Her fury with the programme comes through in her daughter Carol Thatcher's book *Diary of an Election*. She writes that the programme was 'an example of the most crass nastiness and discourtesy shown to a Prime Minister on a television programme'. She quotes in detail one of the 'segments' of the programme—the one about the pensioner's Christmas bonus—but makes no reference to any other topic that was raised.

After the broadcast Ken Stanton and I agreed that we should share a taxi home, as he did not mind the slight detour necessary for him to return to Cheltenham via Cirencester, and of course we chatted about the programme. I must admit that I wondered what my husband, Clifford, would think about my part in it.

He was busy with some school work when I came in, but naturally stopped working and gave me his views. Interestingly enough he had already had a phone call, the first of many, and we found this one rather amusing. An autocratic female voice —she declined to disclose her name—enquired whether she was speaking to someone in the house of the Mrs Gould who had just appeared on 'Nationwide'. She then roundly abused my husband and declared, rather predictably, that we must both be communists! When my husband attempted to get in a word and to explain that we were both practising Christians and ... she abruptly rang off.

Not an Election Issue?

Two days later I had a chance to put a question to the Conservative candidate. The head of Cirencester School had invited the Tory, Labour and Liberal candidates to come to the school at lunchtime on three separate days to put their views to the Sixth Form and Staff and to answer questions. The meetings were held in the Sixth Form Commonroom and of course attendance was entirely voluntary.

Mr Ridley duly came on Thursday, 26 May to deliver his short talk and answer as many questions as was possible in the time available. There were of course questions about cuts in education, especially at university level; unemployment, again of vital importance to the young people in the audience; and the Government's monetary policy in general. I asked him a question about his thoughts on 2 April 1982, in the light of his views expressed in the House in December 1980, and his treatment by the House on that occasion.

I suppose I could hardly have expected him to say that if only the members of Parliament had given him a more sympathetic hearing then, and endorsed the policy of lease-back which he was proposing, the Argentinian invasion would never have occurred! Needless to say he did not reply in this way. He did, however, put forward the view that a few influential members had swayed the rest and that the signal went out to the islanders that they had the wholehearted support of all parties. This signal then gave authority to the hard-liners on the Island and ensured that their views would be of paramount importance.

I had the previous day read the *Guardian* leader entitled 'A Moment of Weakness, Fathoms Deep', which referred to the 'Nationwide' broadcast and the part I played in it. They called me Mrs Diana Gould of Bristol and this 'title' seemed to stick to me in most of the newspaper references. The *Guardian* leader queried first, and then justified, raising the subject as an election issue.

This was a criticism I was getting personally. Cirencester is a very civilised place and therefore those who did not agree with my views, nevertheless did not subject me to any abuse. People would say that they admired my courage in questioning Mrs Thatcher, but that surely it was not an election issue and therefore not a fair question. My answer to them and to anyone else was that in my view it was very definitely an election issue. Mrs Thatcher had said that she was prepared to fight the election on her record in office. That record, I considered, included involving this country in a war which need never have happened. Increasingly throughout her term of office she had developed a presidential style and appeared to wish to take full responsibility for what 'her government' did. Hence my feeling that she, rather than the Conservative Party, should bear the responsibility for all that occurred.

To me, as to many, the war had solved nothing. The new government, when it took over, would still have to deal with the problem of the future of the Falkland Islands. It would also have to find millions of pounds for at least the next few years to maintain Fortress Falklands. Millions of pounds which would have to be spent on 1,800 people when in our own country well over 3 million people were unemployed, cuts were being imposed on all services and more cuts were being forecast and in fact were implemented shortly after the election.

It was also an election issue because the Conservatives

Not an Election Issue?

made it so, in spite of their denials at the time. Many of their candidates were making as much political capital as they possibly could out of the 'Falklands Factor'. Eventually the *Guardian* Diary got an admission from the Conservative Central Office that they had circulated a statement on the Falklands which was used in leaflets and by many of the candidates. This said 'The Falklands War showed our determination to defend freedom and the quality of our armed forces'. They were prepared therefore to make it an election issue and should not have been in any way surprised if those who disagreed with their views also brought it to the notice of the electorate.

Correspondence

The first letter to reach me came from the Hon. George Bathurst, who presumably had recognised me on 'Nationwide' as he and my husband work together on the committee of a Hospital League of Friends. He enclosed a cutting from *The Daily Telegraph* of an article published on Monday, 23 May, the day before the television programme. This article was based on a report written by an American, Dr Robert L. Scheina, in which he claimed that at least three ships of the British Task Force were sailing into the area being patrolled by the *Belgrano* and that one of these was the *Sheffield* which was sunk two days later. A map was shown pinpointing the positions of the two sinkings. It also claimed that the *Belgrano* was not withdrawing to her base at Ushuaia but was steaming at 10 knots up and down a 200-mile long patrol line between Tierra del Fuego and the Burdwood Bank.

In my reply I pointed out that I had not said that the *Belgrano* was sailing home, but that she was sailing on a bearing of 280° away from the Exclusion Zone. I also questioned whether the fact that the *Sheffield* was sunk 180 miles North East of the *Belgrano* two days later gave any information about the position of the *Sheffield* when the *Belgrano* was sunk. The *Sheffield* was capable of a maximum of 29 knots, but I assumed an average of 20 knots, which could have put the *Sheffield's* position any-

Correspondence

where within a range of one nautical mile to 960 nautical miles (20 x 48) from the *Belgrano* at the time of the sinking. I also said that all the Argentinian Navy, including the *Belgrano*, was a threat to our forces wherever it may have been, from the moment our Task Force was despatched. For example, that argument could have been used to justify an attack on their fleet while still in port, and made a nonsense of our Exclusion Zone. In a further letter the Hon. George Bathurst implied that the *Sheffield* and two other ships were involved in a proposed landing of S.A.S. on Tierra del Fuego and were within 30 miles sailing time of the *Belgrano* and therefore many lives were at stake.

I wondered when reading this letter if Mr Bathurst's source of information was the one quoted in the free newspaper that originally involved me in the furore. I wondered if the Cotswold area with its close proximity to G.C.H.Q. at Cheltenham did in fact have access to information denied to Parliament?

I wrote in reply that I found it difficult to believe that he did have such information and he replied that it was in fact merely conjecture on his part. I did also suggest that as the *Conqueror* was shadowing the *Belgrano* the Task Force ships, if they were in the area, could have been alerted and taken evasive action in the vastness of the South Atlantic and that the sailing speed of 10 knots did not suggest that the *Belgrano* was about to make an attack.

It is also strange that the two Argentinian destroyers escorting the *Belgrano* and armed with exocets, did not carry out such an attack on our ships after the sinking if they were outside the Exclusion Zone and in the path of the homeward-fleeing destroyers.

One letter I received attempted to blame the loss of life following the sinking on the fact that the two escorting destroyers had deserted the *Belgrano*. Had they remained to pick up survivors, possibly more might have been saved. But no one can deny that sinking a cruiser in cold Atlantic waters is bound to cause many deaths and had the destroyers stayed they might well have become targets and more lives would have been lost. It is not unlikely that had they remained they would have depth-charged the *Conqueror*. A later report in *The Sunday Times*, again based on writings by Dr Robert L. Scheina, stated that of the three torpedoes fired by HMS *Conqueror* 'two hit the *Belgrano* at range of 1400 yards, third hits forward escort ship but fails to explode'.

The Hon. George Bathurst also asked me to explain why Argentina had any claim to the Falklands. I could not resist suggesting that he had a chat with Mr Nicholas Ridley, his own M.P., whom he would know well. As I pointed out, Mr Ridley wished to educate the Falkland islanders and the people of this country and I was sure he would be delighted to have a discussion.

At about this time I received some correspondence sent on from 'Nationwide' and this included a letter from Mr Michael Woodbine-Parish, the great-grandson of the first British Consul General in Argentina. He deplored the war and hoped for a peaceful settlement with renewed friendship between our two countries. In replying to a query he made I suggested that he might like to get in touch with my previous correspondent who might be interested in the history of Anglo-Argentinian relations.

Letters and phone calls came in from people who had managed to track me down in spite of the 'of Bristol' label I had been given. Some came via 'Nationwide' and the staff there contacted me to ask if they could give my phone number to John Rentoul of the *New Statesman*. We had a very interesting discussion and as a result he sent me a photocopy of the *Daily Mirror* article by Paul Foot (19 May 1983), with a reply by Mr Pym the following day. The article was querying the statement that Mrs Thatcher did not know of the Peruvian Peace Plan until after the sinking of the *Belgrano* and went into great detail about the negotiations. He also sent me a copy of the *New Statesman* of 20 May again on the subject which concedes that the 'text' of the seven-point peace plan may not have reached London until three hours after the sinking but which argued that it was unbelievable Mr Pym and the British Embassy in Washington were not keeping London informed of developments that Saturday and Sunday. So clearly the 'lost hours' that had worried me so much that I had written to 'Nationwide' on 16 May, had also puzzled others far better informed and in touch with international affairs than I, a Gloucestershire housewife.

'Six Hours Away with Exocets'

Nearly a week had gone by since 'On the Spot' had been broadcast and because of the reactions I had received I decided to write to the Labour Party Headquarters, to urge them to make the Falklands into an election issue. A number of letters I had received stated that their writers had always voted Conservative but felt they could no longer do so because of the way in which Mrs Thatcher's government had allowed us to become engaged in such a war and in particular they deplored the loss of life caused by the sinking of the *Belgrano*. Until the sinking there had been virtually no casualties. I hoped the Labour Party would take up the challenge and that I could sink back into obscurity.

As a result, when T.V.A.M. wanted me to appear on their Friday, 3 June programme, I refused to do so. Quite frankly one television appearance was quite enough for me and I really did think the Falklands issue would be taken up officially. In the event, Neil Kinnock had already called for an enquiry, but Mr Dennis Healey's remarks were to prove too emotive and counter productive. When pointing out the hypocrisy of the Conservative Government in the recent financing of the sale of arms, including British arms, to the Argentine dictatorship, he had used the phrase 'glorying in the slaughter' when referring to Mrs Thatcher.

T.V.A.M. had wanted me to comment on a news

'Six Hours Away with Exocets'

programme to be broadcast on Channel 4 on Thursday, 2 June, at 7 p.m. I watched the programme and almost regretted not having taken the opportunity to comment. The query was raised as to why bring up the sinking controversy now. The answer should have been that it was hot news again because of the recent disclosure by Mrs Thatcher that she did not know about the Peruvian Peace Plan until after the action was taken. Mr Heseltine said there had been an enquiry into the Falklands war already and Labour had rejected that. Presumably he was referring to the Franks Report, but this specifically did not include any reference to the conduct of the war, and therefore the sinking of the *Belgrano*, but was concerned with events leading up to the war. Dr David Owen, who had claimed that he had prevented an invasion whilst he was Foreign Secretary in the Labour Government, seemed anxious to defend the conduct of the war by the Conservatives. He pointed out that HMS *Sheffield* was hit soon after the sinking, but as previously shown, in two days she could have been many miles away. The main point to me was Mr Heseltine's statement that the *Belgrano* was within six hours sailing time of the British fleet. This, as I discovered next day, was a reiteration of Mrs Thatcher's statement at a Conservative press conference that morning that the *Belgrano* was an immediate threat to the Task Force as she was 'six hours away with Exocets'.

I wanted to turn this six hours into miles, to discover where our Task Force was, so once again I turned to the local library. They did not have a copy of *Jane's Fighting Ships*, but a phone call to Cheltenham and then to Gloucester produced the information that the *Belgrano's* maximum speed when she was commissioned was 32.5 knots.

Having missed the opportunity to comment on T.V.A.M. I decided to write a letter to the *Guardian*. I pointed out that a speed of 30 knots in 1982 would probably be an over-estimation and therefore the *Belgrano* could at most have covered 180 nautical miles in six hours. Our main fleet had been reported as being over 300 miles away to the North East of the Falklands. The *Daily Telegraph* report (23 May) had stated that the *Belgrano* was patrolling at 10 knots between the Burdwood Bank and Tierra del Fuego and a bearing of 280° would have been consistent with it having turned onto the westward leg of its patrol. I asked again how could the *Belgrano* be an imminent threat to our ships at a time when it was being shadowed by the *Conqueror*, and at a crucial time when a peace plan was under discussion.

I have learned since that the maximum speed of the *Belgrano* was far less than 30 knots. Therefore this reduces its threat even more. Another correspondent has suggested to me that the *Sheffield* was covering a landing by S.A.S. men on the South West side of the Falklands and she was one of the ships threatened. I think this is why the position of the two ships is stressed all the time. But I can only repeat the facts as made known are that the sinkings were 180 miles apart and also two days apart. Did the *Sheffield* stay on station for two days? Moreover, she must have been well within the Exclusion Zone and had the *Belgrano* gone on the attack she would have to have sailed well into the Zone with her destroyer escorts because their Exocets had a range of less than 30 miles. The *Conqueror* shadowing her would then have had every justification, in view of the rules we had made about Argentine ships entering the 200-mile Zone, in sinking her. Also the *Belgrano's* crew, knowing the rules, would have been alert to the danger of an attack and the whole controversy would not have arisen.

A Young Man's Death

The Guardian printed my letter on Tuesday, 7 June and of course gave my address. This led to more letters and phone calls coming in, the great majority being congratulatory and many thanking me for what I had done. Quite a large number asked me to form a pressure group to get an inquiry and promised their support. An old age pensioner said she would willingly do any typing involved. Several people sent me copies of the Ecoropa Information Sheet Eleven entitled *Falklands War, the Disturbing Truth*. Some letters came from people on holiday as far away as Malta and Turkey. One letter, more than all the others, made me feel very sad and after replying and later having a talk on the phone, the writer gave me permission to publish it if I felt it would serve any useful purpose. She wrote it the day she discovered my address and it speaks for itself:

Dear Mrs Gould,

Congratulations on your determined and courageous stand on the programme 'Nationwide', in your persistent questioning of the Prime Minister on the sinking of the *General Belgrano*.

During this election campaign I have been sickened by the arrogance of this woman, and saddened by the sycophantic response she has usually evinced.

My dear nephew Adrian Anslow R.N. aged 20 years

was killed when an Exocet missile, deflected by chaff from the *Invincible* hit the *Atlantic Conveyor* on May 25th. His body was never found. This was said to be in reprisal for the sinking of the *General Belgrano*.

In Adrian's letters home to us he had expressed concern for his enemy, he knew that many were very young and untrained. He expressed also the fervent hope 'that politicians would swiftly come to their senses otherwise a lot of young men were going to die'.

On the day that he died, our close and loving family was shattered.

I well remember the day that Margaret Thatcher became Prime Minister. As a woman I was delighted, although I did not share her political persuasion, I felt that a woman with her traditional caring qualities might change the face of politics. Instead a nightmare has ensued. My sister has lost her only son, my sons their dear friend as a result of war in *1982*!

Nothing will change my opinion that the sinking of the *General Belgrano* was to demolish the chance of peace through negotiation. I have written letters and talked to scores of people without managing to dent or find a chink in the armour of this Boadicea.

You will never know how you helped us all in our frustration and impotence, your articulate and well-informed interrogation of the Prime Minister was a shining light in our present misery.

Well done Diana Gould and thank you.

      Yours sincerely,
      Patricia Potter.

She told me that she had accompanied her sister on the relatives' visit to the Falklands and that all she had seen there merely confirmed her view that the war should never have happened. She hoped that I had not suffered the abuse meted out to her sister for expressing such views. I was horrified to think that anyone in this country could abuse a woman suffering so greatly from the death of her only son.

The Sunday Papers

After writing to *The Guardian* but before the letter was published, I read *The Sunday Times* of 5 June. Normally we take *The Observer* but on this occasion none was available and the newsagent had kept us a *Sunday Times* in place of it. I was therefore able to read a long article headed 'Why the *Belgrano* was Doomed', again based on military research in Argentina by Dr Robert Scheina. To me the article did not explain the reasons for the sinking at all and once again I put pen to paper and wrote to the Editor.

The article asserted that there was one certainty, the submarine *Conqueror* had picked up the *Belgrano* and, by being in the area, it posed a threat. According to Dr Scheina, *Hermes* and six ships were in the North East area of the Exclusion Zone which would have meant they were over 300 miles from the *Belgrano* and had been spotted by an S2 tracker plane flying off the carrier *Veinticinco de Mayo* at about midnight on 1 May. It would therefore appear that if the *Belgrano* were capable of steaming at a maximum of 30 knots she would have taken ten hours to get within striking distance, which I maintained would have allowed time to watch her for a few hours longer since peace talks were still in progress and especially as at the time of the sinking she was actually heading away from the Falklands.

The article also reported that 'both the Foreign Secretary,

Francis Pym, and his junior minister Cranley Onslow have claimed that they were unaware of the state of the Peruvian proposals until after the decision to sink the *Belgrano* had been made'. This decision was taken at a pre-lunch meeting at Chequers. Mrs Thatcher, however, claimed that she did not know of the Peruvian peace plan until after the *Belgrano* was attacked, which was at about 8 p.m. B.S.T., possibly therefore seven hours after the decision was taken and during which time the orders could have been rescinded.

The article stated that the *Conqueror* first sighted the *Belgrano* on the afternoon of 1 May and had tracked it doggedly for thirty hours. The *Belgrano* was sunk at 1457 South Atlantic time on 2 May, thus thirty hours previous to this would be 0900 approximately on 1 May, that is morning not afternoon of course, and even further away from the timing given in the Parliamentary statement 'on 2nd May HMS *Conqueror* detected the Argentine cruiser, *General Belgrano*'.

Two versions of the consultation at Chequers were given and I expressed the hope that Sir Terence Lewin's account was the correct one. I felt that Admiral Woodward's statement that the order to sink was given 'in remarkably short order reputedly in the entrance porch of Chequers', was intended to cheapen still further the deaths of 368 Argentinians.

I concluded with the thought that persists in my mind. Did the *Conqueror* sink the *Belgrano* when it was 45 miles South West of the Burdwood Bank because by then its course was completely obvious: that is, away from the Exclusion Zone? If the attack had been further delayed there would have been no justification whatever to sink her, as desired by the Task Force commanders, and the orders would have had to be withdrawn.

One of the letters I received after Tuesday, 7 May supporting me, asked if I had read the article in the previous Sunday's *Observer* and, if not, offered to send me a photocopy. As no *Observers* were available in our area I contacted the writer of the letter who duly sent me a copy. By the time it arrived on Friday, 10 June the election was over and Mrs Thatcher returned with a landslide majority of seats though not with a majority of votes. One of her first actions was to remove Mr Francis Pym from his post as Foreign Secretary and Mr Cranley Onslow departed from the Foreign Office.

The Observer of 5 June had reported on a telephone conversation its staff had with Alexander Haig, the US Secretary of State at the time of the Falklands War. He said that he did not think the Thatcher War Cabinet had authorised the sinking deliberately to wreck the Peruvian Peace Plan, but that the attack had unquestionably transformed the situation. 'Inevitably, the sinking of the *Belgrano* had a chilling effect on the dialogue, even though the dialogue had not progressed to the point of a breakthrough'.

The newspaper had acquired the transcript of a crucial telephone conversation between the Presidents of Peru and Argentina, together with copies of secret Argentine naval orders. The documents were brought to the paper by Mr Desmond Rice, for five years head of the Royal Dutch Shell Company in Argentina. Captain Hector Bonzo, the *Belgrano's* commander, had told Mr Rice that he set a course of 290° at 0700 hours on 2 May and that he subsequently changed course only once, from 290° to 280°. When torpedoed by the *Conqueror*, the *Belgrano* was only 100 miles from the Argentine coast and had been on a course away from the Task Force and the Falklands for nine hours. These statements could be checked by reading the submarine's log, but this has not been allowed because of 'intelligence secrecy'. If it is a true statement, then it confirms that the *Belgrano* was not an immediate threat to our ships. Captain Bonzo also stated that the maximum crusing speed of the *Belgrano* was 18 knots, far short of the 30 knots I had used in my calculations and it would have taken him 14 hours to cover 250 nautical miles in order to attack our ships. He said that Mrs Thatcher's claim that the *Belgrano* was only six hours from the nearest British surface ship when attacked was absolute nonsense and that he was not zig-zagging.

I wrote a letter to *The Observer* (not published), in which I said I felt that the time factor was of crucial importance. Hence my letter to 'Nationwide' which I had headed 'The Lost Hours'. The time of the sinking of the *Belgrano* was given in Parliament as 1457 South Atlantic time, the version above puts the sinking at nine hours after 0700, that is 1600 hours. The discrepancy is probably because of a 'summer time' element. I pointed out that at least three time-zones were involved, plus the complications of 'summer times'. I asked if someone would put all the facts about the sinking and timing of the Peace Plan into Greenwich Mean Time to clarify the issue. It would be interesting to know if this has been done.

Post-Election

The decision was taken in June 1983, soon after the election, to build a new strategic airfield on the Islands, at a cost of £215m. This clearly confirmed the Government's commitment to its Fortress Falklands policy for the foreseeable future. In the debate in the House, Mr John Silkin, shadow defence spokesman, pointed out that by the time the airfield was completed in 1986, expenditure on the Falklands would be £3m. for each family.

In a discussion on television between Mr Michael Mates, a Conservative MP speaking for the Defence Committee, and Mr George Foulkes, a Labour MP and member of the Foreign Affairs Committee, the former defended the decision to build the airfield on the grounds that to do otherwise would be once again to send the wrong signals to Argentina. He therefore appeared tacitly to admit that Mrs Thatcher's Government, in insisting on the withdrawal of *Endurance* because of cuts in defence expenditure, had indeed sent the wrong signals to the Junta.

In spite of authorising the expenditure of vast sums, the Defence Committee also expressed anxiety about the drain of the Falklands on Britain's NATO defences. The amount of money to be spent on the Falklands was highlighted by the fact that Mr Michael Heseltine, the Defence Secretary, was forced to revise his Defence White Paper within twenty-four hours of its publication when the new Chancellor, Mr Nigel Lawson, insisted on an immediate £500m. cut in public expenditure.

By contrast, the all-party Foreign Affairs Committee did not find Fortress Falklands a viable solution and it pointed out that Argentina's claims to sovereignty over the Falklands on the grounds of Hispanic inheritance and territorial integrity carried more weight in the United Nations than did British claims on the ground of long-standing possession.

On 13 June 1983 *The Guardian* featured an article by Richard Norton-Taylor in which he reviewed an election issue which apparently all parties officially ignored but which had inevitably come to the fore. He had phoned me a few days before and we had had an interesting discussion.

I have read several references to myself in the press and felt when reading them, rather like the patient who lies on the bed apparently unaware, whilst doctors discuss them and their treatment. You wonder if they can really be talking about yourself. This feeling surfaced again when I found my name in the papers because of a disclosure by Sir Robin Day on 31 August at the Edinburgh Festival where, I discovered later, following a showing of 'On the Spot', Mr Tom King MP had called me 'Tam Dalyell in drag'! Sir Robin declared that Mr Michael Foot, the leader of the Labour Party, had told him in a private conversation that Mrs Thatcher had no option but to sink the *Belgrano* and that he did not think it was an election issue and this was agreed by everyone concerned. He revealed this in a debate on the media coverage of the election in which there was criticism that the campaign had been un-provocative and unrepresentative of ordinary life. Mr Foot, however, when contacted issued a statement which recalled that the shadow cabinet had recommended a select committee inquiry and that he was sure that this was the right way to deal with the matter and to have a proper investigation. Such an inquiry has been called for by the leaders of most of the opposition parties. It was authoritatively stated that Mr Foot believed Mrs Thatcher might have been right on the basis of military evidence offered by the Admiralty, but not necessarily right when taking the diplomatic evidence into account of intense activity to sell the Peruvian Peace Plan to Argentina.

Disclosures in the press appear to cast more and more doubts about Mrs Thatcher's lack of knowledge of a viable Peace Plan before the attack on the *Belgrano*. Peru's former Foreign Minister, Dr Arias Stella is reported as contradicting a statement by Mr Francis Pym, that the Peruvians had given no indication that a treaty had been drawn up. Dr Stella, who is now Peru's permanent delegate to the UN in New York, stated that there was nothing at all vague about the seven-point peace proposal, which was entirely consistent with Security Council Resolution 502. This called for the withdrawal of troops from the Falklands and negotiations on the dispute. Dr Stella emphasized that Britain's Ambassador in Lima, Charles Wallace, had been kept fully informed and that President Belaúnde Terry had been in constant and direct telephone contact with Mr Haig whom they thought was in immediate contact with Mr Pym.

It has since been reported that Lord Thomas (Hugh Thomas, the historian and chairman of the Centre for Policy Studies) is said to have had lengthy telephone conversations with key figures in Lima about the Peace proposals which may have by-passed Mr Pym who was officially engaged in discussions with Mr Haig.

Thus we come to the two main questions. Was the *General Belgrano* an immediate threat to our Task Force? Could the decision to sink her have been delayed in the light of the Peace proposals? On the facts which have so far been allowed to emerge the answer to the first question appears to be *no*. The sinking seems to point to a 'bird in hand' policy. Any Argentinian warship at sea was naturally a threat to our Task Force, so one destroyed would lessen that threat. But this attitude makes the establishment of the Total Exclusion Zone a complete irrelevance and perhaps the warning we should have given the Argentinians was that we would sink any of her warships that we discovered at sea.

The responsibility for taking the decision rests fairly and squarely on Mrs Thatcher and her War Cabinet. They were the ones who were supposed to have the overall picture. Here it seems strange that they were prepared to take such a decision without consulting the Foreign Secretary. The explanation given for this was that the War Cabinet had to take decisions even if a member were missing. Such an explanation would be plausible if it had been Mr Cecil Parkinson or Mr William Whitelaw who was absent. But it is difficult to accept when the missing member was the Foreign Secretary at that very time engaged in negotiations for a peaceful settlement.

In considering whether the Argentinians would have agreed to the new plan being advanced by Predisent Belaúnde Terry we must remember two important new factors. One was the decision at last by the United States to align with the British. By 2 May this was an established fact and must have been a grave blow to the Junta. The other was the pre-dawn Vulcan raid followed by the daylight shelling by HMS *Glamorgan*, *Arrow* and *Alacrity* of Port Stanley airfield on 1 May. This surely signalled that we were fully prepared to use our Task Force to combat the invasion.

In the light of the foregoing, did Mrs Thatcher make the wrong decision in giving in to the Admiral's request for permission to sink the Argentinian cruiser, the *General Belgrano*, in the crucial hours of 2 May 1982? Was it another example of her apparent inability to realise the repercussions of her actions in that she did not take into account the effect the sinking would have on the current peace proposals?

Only a full disclosure of all the facts will resolve the questions and these writings are a plea that a full inquiry should be held now — and not in thirty years' time.

Concluded 14 September 1983